594

DEMCO

1997-98 NWMS READING BOOKS

RESOURCE BOOK FOR THE LEADER

IMAGINE THE POSSIBILITIES
Edited by Beverlee Borbe

FOR THE READER

BY GRACE TRANSFORMED
God at Work in Brazil
By Tim Crutcher

ONLY ONE LIFE . . .
The Autobiography of Lorraine O. Schultz
By Lorraine O. Schultz with C. Ellen Watts

JESUS WILL REPAY
By Becky Hancock

THAILAND: LAND OF THE WHITE ELEPHANT
Edited by Jean R. Knox and Michael P. McCarty

TO THE SHELTER
Journeys of Faith in the Middle East
By Kay Browning

WHERE THE RIVER FLOWS
Bringing Life to West Africa
By Linda Seaman

TO THE SHELTER

Journeys of Faith in the Middle East

Kay Browning

Nazarene Publishing House
Kansas City, Missouri

Copyright 1996
by Nazarene Publishing House

ISBN 083-411-6413

Printed in the
United States of America

Cover design: Mike Walsh

All Scripture quotations are from the *Holy Bible, New International Version*® (NIV®). Copyright © 1973, 1978, 1984 by International Bible Society. Used by permission of Zondervan Publishing House. All rights reserved.

10 9 8 7 6 5 4 3 2 1

To my parents, Dean and Dorothy Embick,
who encouraged me to obey and follow God;
to my husband, Lindell,
who led the way;
and to our great kids—
Brittany, Lindsey, Erin, and Reuben—
who have shared and made
the journey wonderful.

Contents

Preface — 9
1. Spiritual Glue — 13
2. The Cedars of Lebanon — 23
3. Never Alone — 31
4. Intifada — 39
5. The Gulf War — 48
6. Trading the Crescent for the Cross — 58
7. Blessed Are the Peacemakers — 66
8. Exiles from Babylon — 71
9. Some Through the Fire . . . — 78
10. Outreach to the Moon — 85
Epilogue — 93

Kay Browning is a missionary, wife, author, and mother of four. She has written a number of articles and curriculum pieces and contributed to other NWMS reading books. She and her husband make their home in Jerusalem.

PREFACE

When a Work and Witness team traveled to the village of Karak, Jordan, a year after the Gulf War, they found scattered around the city Arabic signs pointing to our church. At first they thought these signs said, "Church of the Nazarene." But when a team member asked the pastor of the church, he explained, "The sign simply says, 'To the Shelter.' During the Gulf War the municipality asked the church if our building could be used as a bomb shelter. Mattresses and food supplies were brought in, and signs were put up pointing the way to the church. After the war, we could have taken the signs down, but we decided to leave them up. After all, that's what the church should be—a shelter for everyone."

In an area of the world that bears the scars of both political and spiritual battles, men and women have looked for a place of shelter and safety. King David fled to the cliffs of En Gedi and called on the Lord to protect him. That same Lord has provided shelter to Arab and Jewish believers and to missionaries who have faced heartbreaking trials. They have found refuge under His wings in places such as prisons, bomb shelters, and empty apartments. Unexpected friends have shared their burdens, and unknown Nazarenes have upheld them in prayer. God has not failed them.

He who dwells in the shelter of the Most High
  will rest in the shadow of the Almighty....
"He is my refuge and my fortress,
  my God, in whom I trust" (Ps. 91:1-2).

As the doors of peace crack open, there are new opportunities for the Church of the Nazarene in the Middle East. People there are looking for someone whom they can trust and believe in. The message of the church is one that leads "to the shelter."

Note: Some names of persons and places have been changed to protect identities.

TO
THE
SHELTER

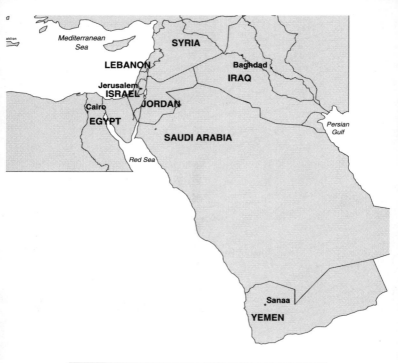

1
Spiritual Glue

BOXES WERE PILED HIGH in our living room. The movers would come again tomorrow to finish packing, and our shipment would begin its long journey to Amman, Jordan. In August 1979, just two months away, we also would travel there to begin Arabic language study. I picked up our 18-month-old daughter, took her to the nursery, and laid her on the changing table. Tears came to my eyes as I looked around the yellow and peach bedroom that we had had so much fun decorating for the new baby. I thought, "Will I ever be this happy again?"

We were moving and changing jobs, and it was robbing us of our sense of stability. It also put to the test our trust in God's plans for our lives. Even though our transition was part of a missionary call, there were still insecurities. I was thankful that our two daughters were small and needed only to be near us to feel secure.

Lindell and I had been married five years and had lived four of those years in Anderson, Indiana. After finishing seminary, Lindell worked as youth pastor for Anderson First Church of the Nazarene.

Those were wonderful, happy years. Our daughters Brittany and Lindsey had been born during our time there, and the church had enveloped us with love and made us feel like family. They understood that we had been preparing ourselves to be missionaries ever since we were teenagers, and that God had called us, but it was still going to be difficult to leave them. The congregation gave us a generous deputation offering and promised to support us with prayer.

Our families had also been supportive, even when they learned our assignment was to "Arabic language study" somewhere in the Middle East. When I told my dad where we had been assigned, his chin quivered, and in a disturbed voice he said, "That's the hot spot of the world." He obviously had been more attentive to world events and knew more than we did about where we would be going. Granted, we had not expected to be sent there, but it sounded OK to us. We would just avoid the troubled spots, and nothing would happen.

Bidding farewell to our families was the most difficult part of leaving. I remember saying those final good-byes and having the impression that something would happen to my mother, that I might not see her again. I tried to shake away that feeling, for we had a long journey to make. Our hearts ached as we made those farewells.

Lindell and I sat down on the plane and shared the secret fears we each had. I admitted my own fear of living in the Middle East, and Lindell confessed to me his feelings of insecurity and inadequacy. The unknown future seemed like a monster ready to swallow us. Then we remembered the wall plaque we had given my mother just before we left. On it were written the words "God's will does not take us where His grace cannot keep us."

The journey to our new home was not an easy one. When we flew out on August 27, 1979, our itinerary included a stopover in Cyprus, a small island in the Mediterranean Sea. The eight Nazarene missionaries in the Middle East were meeting there for a time of fellowship and planning, and they had requested that we join them. After two days together, it was time for us to continue our trip to Amman with Gordon and Pat Johnston, our Nazarene missionaries living in Jordan.

We arrived at the Cyprus airport an hour before departure, only to be told that we couldn't board because the airplane was on the runway ready to take off. The departure time had been moved forward an hour, and we had not been notified. Our only option was to exchange our tickets for a flight two days later and spend two nights in a hotel near the airport. Unfortunately, there was no direct flight to Amman, and we had to make a connecting flight in Beirut. That was the one place in the Middle East we didn't want to go. God obviously had other plans.

On Wednesday, we arrived at the airport more than two hours early. The flight was overbooked, but we were assigned seats and told to pass through security clearance. While waiting to board the plane, an announcement was made that our flight was delayed due to a strike in the Beirut airport. An hour later, we were told we could board the plane. Lindell and I eagerly gathered our numerous pieces of carry-on luggage and our squirming daughters and then headed across the hot tarmac to climb the steep stairs of the aircraft. Just moments after we sat in our seats, the airline attendant apologized as she informed us we would have to disembark. The strike was on again, and the plane could not land in Beirut.

After another hour of waiting in the airport lounge, the welcome announcement came—Beirut passengers could board the plane again. This time we settled in the airplane and breathed a sigh of relief as the flight took off. After half an hour in the air, the aircraft made a sharp turn. We were headed back to Cyprus. The Beirut airport was again on strike, and we could not continue our journey. As we waited in the now-familiar departure area, we wondered if we would ever get to Beirut.

It was another 30 minutes before we were told yet again to board the plane. We sat down and buckled our seat belts, doubting that the plane would ever take off. To our surprise, about an hour later we finally landed in Beirut. Predictably, we missed the connecting flight to Amman, which had departed on schedule, and there was no other flight until the next day. Despite our pleas for permission to stay in Lebanon, armed soldiers escorted us back to the airplane we had just left because we didn't have the necessary visas. The airline, of course, was happy to sell us a return ticket to Cyprus. As we looked forlornly at Gordon and Pat Johnston, all they could say was, "Welcome to missionary life in the Middle East."

Another day was spent in Cyprus before we finally left on a direct flight to Amman. We were so happy to get off the plane and settle down somewhere. Amman became the most beautiful city we had ever been in—never mind if our new apartment had little furniture and a skimpy water supply. Our sense of adventure carried us through days of adjustment, and God's call upon our lives gave those days purpose.

It wasn't long, however, until the excitement wore off and our family faced homesickness. I would sneak away to the bedroom to cry so my husband and daughters wouldn't see me. Later I learned that Lindell did the same thing. But we knew that homesickness wasn't fatal, and soon we were feeling better. By the time General Superintendent V. H. Lewis came in October for the district assembly, we were ready to hear his words of challenge. We were admonished to stick with it, learn the language, and keep God's goals in mind. Lindell and I were no longer looking backward but ahead.

Just a few days after Dr. and Mrs. Lewis left Amman, a message came for me to call home immediately. We didn't have a telephone in our home because there was a two-year waiting list, and my family had made several phone calls before they got ahold of someone who could contact us. At eight o'clock in the morning we bundled up our girls and headed to the district office, where we could place a call to my family in Illinois. After two hours of waiting, an overseas line opened up, and we made contact with my sister.

She explained that our mother had developed an aneurysm on the optic nerve and had suddenly gone blind. She had been rushed to a hospital for surgery. The operation had lasted over 7 hours, and Mother had not regained consciousness in the 20 hours since. There was the possibility that she might not live. If she did live, she might be blind or have severe brain damage.

I hung up the phone with a feeling of helplessness and shock. This couldn't be happening. We had just left family to serve God as Nazarene missionaries. The hurt was almost unbearable, yet I felt God's sustaining presence and knew that people in the United States and in Amman were praying for us.

When we telephoned my family two days later, we learned that my mother's condition had worsened. She had not regained consciousness after the surgery, and there was swelling in her brain. After two more days, a call came from my oldest brother, telling us that Mother's condition was critical and that the doctors needed to perform more surgery to remove the pressure on her brain. The specialists made no promises; they simply told the family that the surgery was her only chance of survival.

Lindell and I knew the time had come for me to go home to my family. Before we drove to the airport, Lindell wanted to see the pastor of the church we attended. The news had already reached Brother

David Nazha, and he greeted us with sympathy and understanding. He expressed his concern and asked if he could pray for me and my mother.

In a booming voice with words of a language I barely understood, he began to pray. Although we stood in a circle facing each other, it was as though he picked up my wounded spirit and lifted me to the Father. I realized then that part of our lives were being intertwined with these people of the Middle East. Through the years their suffering had been great. They had much to teach me, and I had much to learn.

In just 48 hours, God had helped us work out the arrangements for me and Lindsey to be on our way to St. Louis. During the 20-hour flight I prayed that my mother would not die and that she would know I had come back. My younger brother met us at the airport and brought us the news that Mother had survived surgery and was starting to come out of her coma. Part of my prayer had been answered.

We went directly to the hospital and entered my mother's room. There was little about the person in the bed that looked like my mother. The operation had left her head shaven, bruised, and swollen to twice its normal size. Wires and tubes connected her to life-saving machines. But when I placed my hand in hers and said, "Hi, Mom—it's Kay," there was a gentle squeeze that let me know she had recognized me. The second part of my prayer had been answered.

The doctors were reluctant to make any predictions about Mother's recovery. She had suffered a stroke during the period between the two surgeries, leaving her left side paralyzed. There was brain damage, and her vision was limited. I stayed with my family almost six weeks, spending most of that time at the hospital. Gradually Mother was able to talk, and some of her strength returned.

When the decision was made to move Mother to a rehabilitation center, I knew it was time for me to return to my husband and daughter in Jordan. My family was hopeful that with intensive therapy Mother would be able to return home in a few months. It was difficult to say good-bye again, especially to my father. But he understood that I had to follow God's direction for my life, and he realized that my own family needed me too. I returned to Jordan and worked diligently at trying to catch up in my language studies.

Two months later another phone call came. Mother had suffered seizures for several hours and gone into a deep coma. The doctors said she might remain in a coma for days, months, or even years. This time I did not return and tried my best to focus on the task of learning Arabic.

Despite my diligence, I was not very successful as more distractions and obstacles arose. During our second year Brittany had hepatitis while I was pregnant with our third child. When the doctor diagnosed Brittany's illness, he stringently warned me to be careful, since hepatitis was extremely dangerous during the first three months of pregnancy. The physician gave me a long list of "things not to do" in order to avoid getting sick, but I had already done them all. Knowing that hepatitis was highly contagious, we again called upon the family of Arab believers to pray for us. After a few weeks passed, we knew God had heard those prayers. Six months later, a healthy baby girl, whom we named Erin Elizabeth, was born.

The months stretched into another year, and my mother remained in a coma. There was nothing we could do but pray for her and my family at home, who carried such a heavy burden. A month after Erin was born, we moved to Nazareth, Israel, where Lindell began supervision of the Nazarene work there and in the area of Galilee. The people of our new church were loving and concerned, and they began to help us carry the burden for my mother and family. After hearing my concern for the financial burden my father faced, one young woman suggested we bring them to Nazareth so they could help us take care of them.

Just 20 months after Erin was born, I gave birth to our son, Reuben David. When our first furlough came in 1983, we returned, eager to show off two new babies. But that excitement was overshadowed by the need to see my mother. After a year and a half, she had come out of the coma but had suffered severe brain damage. This time when I went to her hospital room, she didn't know me. Eyes that were clouded over with cataracts showed no sign of recognition. With a broken heart, I left the room muttering the word "Why?" My mother was to remain in that same condition until she died 10 years later.

God listened to my question and eventually gave me a release from the burden of needing to know. The promise of Phil. 4:11-13 took on new meaning in my life. I discovered the peace that God could give in all circumstances. He taught me that there can be contentment even without ecstatic happiness, and He helped me realize that He understands and feels our hurts and sorrows with us. I once heard contentment described as "peace that doesn't fall to pieces." It is the spiritual glue that holds us together.

We returned to Nazareth after a year of furlough, renewed by the prayers and encouragement we felt as we visited Nazarene churches in the United States. Farewells were again difficult, the Middle East was still unstable, but we were ready to return and see what God's future held for us.

2
THE CEDARS OF LEBANON

OUR FIRST CHRISTMAS overseas was a bittersweet one. I had just returned from spending almost six weeks with my family during the initial crisis with my mother. Despite the concern for my family in the United States, I was eager to get back to my husband and daughters. Lindell had been a wonderful "Mr. Mom" and had even managed to unload the crates that had arrived with all our personal belongings. I knew he was eager to travel and learn more about the Nazarene work in the Middle East, so when I got home, I encouraged him to make a trip to Lebanon with Gordon Johnston during our Christmas break from language school.

It was 1979, and the civil war that was destroying this beautiful country had been in progress about six years. Nazarene missionaries had stayed as long as possible, but in 1975 the United States State Department required all American citizens to leave Lebanon. Gordon and Pat Johnston relocated to Jordan, where Gordon continued to direct the work in Lebanon. As often as possible, Gordon traveled back to Beirut to encourage the people and check on the condition of our churches and school.

Lindell's first visit to Lebanon took him through the streets of a city divided and controlled by various militia groups. As he and Gordon drove down roads lined with soldiers, tanks, and checkpoints, it was difficult to discern who was on whose side. They met with our church members, who lived under the threat of bombs and bullets and who often had to seek protection in bomb shelters when the fighting became intense. Although a temporary truce was in effect during the time of their visit, it was obvious this war would not soon be over.

The next 11 years brought more devastation and despair. It became impossible for American missionaries to make even short visits into Lebanon. Americans and Europeans continued to be kidnapped and held as hostages, and missionaries had been among those taken. It was not until 1991 that Lindell and I returned there. The fighting militia groups had finally signed a peace agreement, and we were given special permits to visit the country.

Our journey to Beirut began in Damascus, Syria. We traveled overland by bus across beautiful mountains and through the Baka Valley. Our guide pointed out that it was likely some of the hostages were still being held in the villages through which we passed. Ironically, it was safe enough for us to stop and buy a quick lunch in one of the friendly village shops. However, when we arrived in Beirut, we slept in a convent situated in the mountains overlooking the city, rather than in a hotel. Security precautions were still necessary.

The only way to get to Beirut from the convent was by a chaotic, 40-minute drive down the mountains. In a city overcrowded with cars, there were few functioning traffic lights and even fewer frustrated traffic police. The devastation to the city was indescribable. In the center of Beirut was a 10-mile circle in which nothing remained but shells of collapsed buildings.

From a population of just over 3 million people, there had been 150,000 deaths. One-third of the inhabitants had been displaced, often moving from one safe place to another. But statistics don't tell the stories of tragedy and hardship that people have endured. One taxi driver told us that he and his family had survived by driving their vehicle to the mountains and making their car their home.

During the years of conflict, communication with our Lebanese church leaders was nearly impossible. Since Americans had been forbidden to make even short visits to the country, our Lebanese Nazarenes had little access to anyone connected with the rest of their international family. Despite the hardships and struggles, however, our two churches and our Nazarene school in Beirut managed to keep their doors open. The school was located in an area where heavy fighting had taken place during the latter years of the war. Buildings on both sides had been hit by bombs, and the shattered walls crumbled down on the school. The whole area had been without electricity for months at a time. But God honored the faith and determination of the Lebanese Nazarenes, and the schools and churches survived the civil war.

The director of the Beirut Nazarene school was a man named Abdu Khanashat. When we visited him during that 1991 trip, he was eager for us to see the restoration that had been made possible by a grant from Nazarene Compassionate Ministries. The freshly plastered and painted walls stood in contrast to the bullet-ridden, shattered structures surrounding the school. Abdu told us how the adults and young people of the church had helped repair the buildings. He then took us to the basement bomb shelter that had provided safety for hundreds of people during the bomb attacks. After the restoration was completed, sewing machines and tables had been brought in to provide income-generating work for the community.

As Abdu showed us the shelter, he directed our attention to the corner where a simple, concrete container shaped like a large tub stood about four feet high. Brother Khanashat explained that the concrete tub was a baptistery. Just a few weeks earlier, the church had held a special service of praise and celebration in which seven people were baptized. Where else could one find a baptistery in a bomb shelter except in Beirut?

From the basement we went to the roof, where Abdu showed us the new electric generator. The still-frequent power blackouts would no longer interrupt the school's operation. But what caught our eyes was a four-foot metal frame shaped like a cross. Bullet holes had shattered the opaque plastic that had at one time covered the structure; but even though the cross was badly damaged, it had remained standing. It stood as a symbol of these Beirut Christians, invincible in the midst of overwhelming difficulties.

Abdu drove us to his apartment for a meal and fellowship with his family. As we traveled, he began to tell us the story of a time when he faced great despair and discouragement. Fierce fighting had begun in the neighborhood of the school. Knowing parents would be worried about their children, the staff put the boys and girls into the tattered school buses and hurried them to their homes. Abdu loaded his car with the children who couldn't be squeezed on the buses. He then returned to the school to wait for his 17-year-old daughter, who was at a school 10 miles away. Because of the fighting, her school bus refused to deliver her to the Nazarene school. Abdu wanted to leave immediately to get her, but his daughter's school said it was too dangerous for him to travel at that time.

By noon there were people everywhere, carrying whatever possessions they could hold. Bombs and explosives of all kinds filled the air with noise. People living close to the school came running with their blankets and food. They held the hands of their weeping and screaming children and led them to the safety of the school's bomb shelter. Soon the streets were empty except for soldiers preparing their cannons and weapons for the next battle. Electrical lines were cut and the water turned off.

Smoke covered the area, and darkness fell over the city. At five o'clock another battle began.

Abdu carried a candle to a small, dark room in the shelter. Outside, it sounded like a rainstorm as the shooting, bombing, and shelling commenced again. He entered the gloomy room, knelt down, and began to pray. "O my Lord, what shall I do? What do You want me to do? I'm away from my family, and I don't know if they are alive. Would You please keep them safe? The war may last for days, and who will take care of them? Who will feed me? Give me some promises from Your Word."

God answered: "Listen, Abdu! Aren't you My son? Don't you trust your Father to whom you are praying every day? Didn't I feed Elijah in the desert?"

At that moment someone knocked at the door. Abdu opened it, and in front of him stood an old man with a dishful of food and bread. He said he knew Abdu hadn't eaten all day and asked him to accept this food from him. With tears in his eyes, Abdu gratefully accepted the food. The simple gift reassured Abdu that God had not forgotten nor forsaken him.

After eight days in the shelter, the bombing stopped. The people ventured outside and found that the school had become the border between the two warring parties. As soon as possible, Abdu went to his daughter's school. He found her well but worried. Together they began to look for the rest of the family. When they reached home, no one was there. Their apartment complex had been hit, and the building was surrounded by ruined houses and burning fires. None of the neighbors knew where Abdu's wife, daughter, son-in-law, and one-year-old grandson were. They returned to the school with heavy hearts but praying and trusting God that the family would be found alive. After several days, Abdu and his daughter rejoiced as they learned the rest of the family was safe and unharmed. All told, it was a month before they were finally reunited.

Abdu's story ended just as we arrived at his apartment, located in the mountains overlooking the sea. He explained that his family had moved away from the city to avoid the ever-increasing battles, and yet some of the last fighting of the war took place in this area.

As he showed us his recently repaired apartment, we noticed a freshly plastered wall in one of the bedrooms. Abdu explained that a bomb had crashed through the wall and landed unexploded on the bed. Only minutes before, his grandson had been lying on the bed. Again, he praised God for the protection of his family.

We left Abdu's home amazed at his family's courage and strength. They and many like them did not lose their faith in God nor their hope for a better future. As we said good-bye to the people we had met in homes, churches, and schools, they thanked us for coming and encouraging them. Lindell and I were deeply touched.

The people of our churches reminded us of a wall poster with a picture of the beautiful Beirut harbor. On it are written the words "Beirut—a city that will not surrender." Our Nazarenes had not surrendered their faith in God nor their love for their church. Like the cedars of old, they stand firm, they stand tall, and they offer their country a beautiful fragrance—the fragrance of Christ.

3

NEVER ALONE

EDUCATION IS IMPORTANT to families in the Middle East. It did not take me long to understand this. During the time of final exams, some students would literally go into isolation as they intensely studied. In the early 1980s, Arab students wanting to attend college often went outside their homeland, because their universities were full. Of course, this was expensive, but there were various political and social organizations that provided scholarships.

On one of our first visits to a church in southern Jordan, we met a young man who was preparing to study in a neighboring country. Rasheed was anxious to pursue a degree in agricultural engineering, but he was also eager to attend the strong Nazarene church in the country to which he was moving. On a previous visit Rasheed had found this church full of adults but lacking young people. Since his home church was full of teens, he felt God leading him to begin youth meetings and encourage young people to attend the regular services of his newly adopted church.

Rasheed was able to rent an apartment in his new country with some of his cousins and settled into the life of a student. Although there were only a few born-again Christians at his school, he was able to find a student fellowship for believers at another college in the city.

Rasheed's first two years passed quickly. He enjoyed studying in his classes, attending the church, and helping with the youth work. During the summer he was able to return to Jordan and tell his church about the blessings he had received as he helped in the churches. The scholarship money for his education was renewed, and the only expectation the sponsoring organization had was that he do well in his studies.

Rasheed had no trouble balancing his studies and his work in the church. The youth were growing in the Lord and were involved in lay witness training. Sometimes Rasheed would go out with two other young men, and he would witness while they watched and prayed. The youth were taught how to witness so they would be ready to share their faith. Young people from the church were also involved in hospital visitation.

After one such visit, Rasheed and his coworkers took a taxi home and began a discussion about their faith, well aware that another passenger in the taxi was listening to every word. The stranger joined in the discussion. They learned he was also living outside his homeland while he studied. The passenger asked many questions, some of which aroused a bit of suspicion in Rasheed and made him feel uneasy. But when the fellow traveler asked Rasheed if he would meet him again to discuss religion, he agreed. The young believers were encouraged and excited about the witnessing opportunity the Lord had given them.

The next day, five of his friends went with Rasheed to the meeting place, anxious to pray and share their faith. Rasheed remembered the taxi ride of the day before and tried to shake away a feeling of uneasiness. Some of the questions that had been asked were very personal and almost seemed prying, so he was glad to have his friends with him. After a warm greeting, the young people began talking.

During the discussion, an outsider approached the group and asked to talk privately to their new friend. It became obvious that these two men were previously acquainted. The believers encouraged the stranger to join them, but he pulled his friend aside and asked Rasheed to join him instead. Reluctantly, Rasheed left, but after a few steps he realized he had forgotten his books and turned back to get them. As he turned, three more men with guns approached and forced him to continue walking. There was no way he could resist.

At first Rasheed thought they merely wanted to question him in some private place. Then they blindfolded him and took him to an office used by one of the political parties. He recognized the name of the group as the organization that was providing his scholarship. They brought him coffee and told him to wait.

After two hours an official of the party came, asked where Rasheed was, and ordered that he be taken to another place. The three assailants carried him out of the room and forced him into a car. Another man joined them, and the five squeezed into the backseat. In the front seat was the officer who had ordered the transfer. He flung his gun toward Rasheed and hit him on the legs. Rasheed began to pray.

The car stopped at the secret police building, and Rasheed was shoved into a prison cell that held two other prisoners. Guards took all his personal items, including his eyeglasses and belt. The hours passed, and the cold night came. There was no bed, pillow, or blankets in the room, so Rasheed used his shoes for a pillow and tried to rest on the cement floor. Finally sleep came.

At midnight the guards woke Rasheed and took him away for questioning. He was bound in chains and again blindfolded. During the interrogation they suggested he make it easy on himself and admit his involvement with another political party. He refused to confess to this lie, so the guards beat him before taking him back to his prison cell. In the early morning hours he was questioned and beaten two more times. One time they ordered Rasheed to undress before they beat him. After striking him, they alternately poured hot water and cold water over his body.

His physical and emotional strength gone, Rasheed began to cry and agreed to answer their questions. He explained that he belonged to a church, not a political party. He was a Christian, but apparently this answer was not acceptable. Rasheed's captors continued to beat him until his resistance broke down. After the beatings stopped, he was escorted back to his cell, only to be taken away a few hours later to sign documents of confession.

Rasheed's spirit was broken; he felt guilty and ashamed that he had agreed to statements that weren't true. He couldn't even recall all that he had told them. They had been successful, and he had been defeated. For three days the guards left him alone, and Rasheed spent that time praying and asking God to forgive him for his weakness and inability to stand strong in his faith. God touched his heart and body, and Rasheed felt the presence of the Lord in his place of imprisonment.

Guards moved Rasheed to another prison, which was actually a dungeon without windows or outside light. About 50 other political prisoners were housed in the crowded jail. The physical abuse continued. Soon the other prisoners noticed a difference in the way Rasheed reacted to his beatings. They came back cursing and crying, but Rasheed returned calmly and quietly to his place in the cell. This silent testimony provided opportunities for him to witness and pray with some of the inmates.

Once a Muslim sheik who had just been beaten asked Rasheed to pray with him. He seized hold of Rasheed and insisted he pray. In a room filled with Muslims, Rasheed wondered how he could do this. He suggested they pray later, in private, but the sheik insisted Rasheed pray then and there. Rasheed shook away his fears and told the sheik he would pray, but that he too could pray to Jesus. This was the first of several opportunities Rasheed had to pray with this man.

Conditions in the prison were deplorable. It was dark and dirty, and ants floated in the drinking water. Meals consisted of bread and rice, but there was never enough food for everyone. The prisoners were forced to have their heads shaved, and they were constantly humiliated.

When the prisoners heard the rattling of the keys, it was the signal for them to stand on one foot and put their hands above their head. The guards would then make a sadistic game of selecting someone for a beating. They were allowed to use the toilet only once a day, and as the guards walked them down the hall, they were beaten with a stick. The captors did everything they could to break the spirit of the imprisoned men, and it wasn't long before the prisoners began to fight among themselves.

During one time of questioning, the interrogating officer began to talk to Rasheed about Jesus Christ. He asked Rasheed if he believed Jesus was the Son of God. When Rasheed answered yes, the guard replied, "If Jesus is the Son of God, why did God allow Him to be crucified?" Rasheed tried to explain that Jesus was crucified for our sins; and although He died on the Cross, He rose again. Only the Son of God could do that. Rasheed told him that Jesus had died for us all. The guard continued to taunt Rasheed with his questions. This in itself was not unusual, but seldom did the guards ask about Jesus.

After more questioning, the officer stared silently at Rasheed. He then told Rasheed he would like to give him the opportunity to suffer as Jesus did. He told Rasheed to remove his clothes and ordered the guards to bring a ladder, blindfold, and chain. With eyes blindfolded, Rasheed was chained to the ladder as if he were being crucified. They dragged the ladder into the hallway and placed it next to the torture room. For six hours Rasheed hung on the ladder and endured the jabs and blows of guards as they passed by him. God gave Rasheed the strength to endure this humiliating punishment, and his spirit remained strong.

Rasheed was concerned about his family, for he knew they would be worried about him. He prayed that the friends who had been with him when he was taken away would get information to his family and church. He knew they would pray for him, and he drew strength from that knowledge.

One day Rasheed was moved out of the dungeonlike prison and put into a jail with barred windows. For many hours he tried to get the attention of a lady living in a nearby house. Finally he succeeded and gave the neighbor a piece of paper with his name and the name and phone number of his cousin. The lady took the information and contacted his cousin. A believer who lived in a house next to one of the guards discovered where Rasheed was being held. He paid the guard to take a few items to Rasheed. Those simple gifts lifted Rasheed's spirits, and he was again reminded that God had not forgotten him.

The days of imprisonment stretched into weeks, then a month, but it was difficult to keep track of time. Without a Bible, books, or even a clock, Rasheed's days were long and dreary. When new prisoners were brought in, the others immediately asked, "What's the date?" But for Rasheed, God turned those dark, depressing days into days of sweet fellowship with Him. He began to sing songs of praise and spent much of the time praying and fasting. God had become his close Companion.

Eventually, some of the guards became less cruel, and a few were even friendly. One of them secretly told him he would be released soon. After 56 days of imprisonment, Rasheed was set free. He was taken to the border and released without his passport or identification papers. As he crossed the border, he prayed that they would let him back into the country without those important documents. The authorities at the border listened to his story and welcomed him to his homeland. In a few hours, Rasheed was home with his family. After a happy reunion and much rejoicing, he went to the church to thank the congregation for their prayers. There was a great time of celebration for several days.

Today Rasheed seldom talks about his prison stay; he refers to it as his "wilderness experience." Years have passed since those days of suffering and pain. Rasheed is married now and is studying for the ministry. Though that does not promise to be an easy course for his life, he has learned that however much he is tempted and tested, God will never leave him alone.

4
INTIFADA

THE ARAB CITY of Nazareth was our home in the Middle East from 1981 to 1988. Our family lived in a complex that included a garden, parsonage apartment, church, and preschool building. It was a wonderful place to live, and we felt settled and secure. Although there were occasional terrorist attacks in Israel, nothing happened in Nazareth except an occasional bomb scare.

During that time, we were virtually unaware of the tensions that were growing stronger and stronger on the West Bank. We often drove through the West Bank cities of Janin, Nabulus, and Ram Allah on the way to Jerusalem. Nazarene missionaries Earl and Norma Morgan and Chris and Susan Grube told us that the dissension between the Palestinians and Israelis was growing stronger. Life in Jerusalem was becoming more and more stressful, and they feared something major was going to happen.

In December 1987 the Palestinian *intifada* or "uprising" began, in which the Palestinian Arabs protested the occupation of the West Bank by the Israeli government. The unrest started in an Arab area called Gaza and spread to other West Bank cities. A few days later, violent rioting began; Israeli soldiers were injured, and several Arabs were killed. Citizens of Nazareth decided to show their solidarity with the Palestinians and planned a demonstration on the main street of town.

Expecting nothing but a peaceful demonstration, Lindell took our older daughters for their two-hour violin lessons in a city about 35 miles north of Nazareth. I remained home with Erin, Reuben, and Rami, an eight-year-old foster boy living with us at that time. Schools were dismissed early and children sent home as a strange quietness fell over the city.

At one o'clock in the afternoon, churches were to ring their bells as a sign of respect for those who had been killed or injured in the riots of the past two days. As the bells were ringing, I looked out the second-floor window of our apartment and realized that the big iron gates in the garden had not been closed. Before I turned to go down the stairs, a gray police bus stopped in front of the gates and driveway, and 50 border police, outfitted in full riot gear, began to descend from the bus.

The children and I stepped onto the living room balcony to watch what was happening. From there I climbed onto the flat roof of the church and realized that the riots were moving from the center of town toward our buildings. Young men were running in the streets, throwing stones, burning tires, and pushing flaming garbage cans into the path of the police, who were hurling tear gas canisters at the rioters.

Despite the danger, I decided to leave the front gates open in case Lindell and the girls needed to quickly drive the van into the garden when they returned. I then decided to try to occupy the children in some other activity. Rami was happy to play games with Reuben and Erin, but he was also very curious about the events happening in front of the church. After getting the children settled and distracted, I returned to some work that needed to be finished. I was busy in a back room when someone cried out, "Mommy!"

Rushing to the living room, I found all three children huddled together on the outside balcony. I looked down and saw what had frightened them. In a corner of the garden, police had caught some teenage boys and were hitting them with sticks as they dragged them out of the garden. As soon as they left, I rushed out of the room to shut the garden gates. On the stairs I met a young man running toward our door, obviously looking for a place to hide. I could envision police chasing him into our house and didn't hesitate for a moment to tell him to leave and get out of our garden. Our children had seen more than enough that day. He climbed over the fence and disappeared.

As darkness came, the rioting ended, and Lindell returned with Brittany and Lindsey. They had driven around burning tires to get home but arrived safely. Although Christmas was just a few days away, we knew it would not be a peaceful one in Israel.

That incident started a very violent, troubled

time within the boundaries of Israel and in the Arab areas occupied by Israeli authorities. The troubled spots continued to be Gaza, the West Bank, and Jerusalem, but not Nazareth, so our daily lives were unaffected. However, when we went to Jerusalem, we no longer traveled through the Judean hills and West Bank cities.

Our churches in Jerusalem were forced to cancel evening services. An outreach Sunday School in a West Bank village had to stop because stones were thrown at the car taking our Sunday School workers there. Protest strikes were called once or twice a week, forcing the closures of schools and business places. Our missionaries in Jerusalem told us it was difficult for them to avoid troubled areas. Susan and Chris Grube found themselves in a precarious situation when soldiers forced entry into their house, looking for a neighbor who had thrown stones. Life in the Holy Land began to change.

In the fall of 1989 our family moved to Jerusalem. Earl and Norma Morgan were retiring, and the Grube family was leaving to the United States for furlough. Needless to say, it was a major change for us. Although Nazareth was a city with 80,000 people, it felt like a village. Jerusalem, however, was the political and spiritual hub of the country. We experienced the increasing stress and danger of the intifada and tried to adjust our lives to the uncertainty it created.

Over the next few years, the violence of the intifada continued to increase. It was not unusual for cars parked in front of our church to have windows smashed by the angry youth in the neighborhood. The stoning of passing cars continued. Every day at least two or three parked cars were burned by angry arsonists. Once while our children were in a church meeting with friends, the car in which they had ridden was set afire. We felt very vulnerable.

In early 1991 we moved from Jerusalem to a larger and cheaper apartment in Bethlehem. Although we lived just beyond the city limits of Jerusalem, our home was located on the West Bank. And the atmosphere there was much different. We encountered a spirit of despair, hopelessness, and fear among our Palestinian neighbors.

We had not realized the strain they had lived under during the years of the intifada. Jobs were scarce, political pressures great, and daily living full of uncertainties. Sometimes we would help a worried neighbor look for a son who had not returned home after a day's work. If a young Palestinian man was anywhere near the scene of a car stoning or similar incident, he would be taken by the military for questioning, and it might be days before he would be released. We would pray with our neighbors and do what we could to help their situation.

Our daily trips into Jerusalem took us on the main road into the city through an area where stones were frequently thrown at passing cars. If a car was licensed by the Israeli government, the car had yellow car plates. Angry youths would hide behind buildings and aim stones at such cars. Our minivan was one of these vehicles. We knew the yellow tags made us a potential target, but we put a sign in our window that said "Church of the Nazarene," hoping that the young men would not stone our car.

Months earlier, when Lindell and I had been driving by a Palestinian refugee camp, a large stone hit our windshield and sent slivers of glass over our clothes. Fortunately, neither one of us was hurt. We reassured ourselves that it wouldn't happen again and continued our daily trips in and out of Jerusalem.

Even though many people were afraid to travel on the West Bank, our children had friends who would come to visit. Usually we provided transportation to and from our home. Such was the case one Saturday in October 1991.

Just as it became dark, we loaded our van with three of our kids and four of their friends and drove toward Jerusalem. As we went down the main road and passed a stone quarry, we heard a loud thud. A large stone had hit our van. Immediately one of the children cried out, "Something hit me!" Our eldest daughter quickly moved to the backseat and saw that Reuben had been hit by a stone. Blood was pouring from the gash in the back of his head. We stopped momentarily, then sped away from the West Bank to a friend's house close by.

The cut was deep, and we needed to get Reuben to the hospital. Our friend Salim, an Israeli Arab fluent in both Hebrew and English, took Lindell and Reuben to Hadasseh Hospital. I stayed with Salim's wife and the rest of the children and cleaned the glass from the car.

All of us were distressed and concerned. How could this happen to us? Stories of deaths due to stone injuries flashed through my mind. If Reuben had not turned away from the window while he was talking to his friend, the stone would have hit his eye instead of the back of his head. We shuddered as we thought of the serious injury that might have occurred.

On the way to the hospital, eight-year-old Reuben kept asking, "Am I going to die?" His shirt was covered with blood, and the wound continued to bleed. Lindell did his best to calm him. Finally a pale, upset Reuben returned with Lindell and Salim, and Lindell told us what had happened at the hospital.

The cut had needed eight stitches, but X rays revealed that there was no concussion. As the doctor stitched Reuben's head, Lindell stood near, assuring him that everything would be all right. While Lindell was holding Reuben's left hand, he noticed Reuben staring at his right hand and moving his fingers.

Lindell became worried, thinking something else might be wrong, so he asked Reuben if his hand hurt. Reuben told his father that he was just trying to do what Dad had taught him. He responded, "Dad, remember you said that whenever we felt afraid, we should look at our right hand and think about the verse Isa. 41:13?" Reuben had been silently repeating those comforting words as he looked at his hand:

> *For I am the LORD, your God,*
> *who takes hold of your right hand*
> *and says to you, Do not fear;*
> *I will help you.*

The next morning I picked up the bloodstained T-shirt, intending to throw it away. Instead, I decided to soak the shirt in a new stain remover. When I checked the shirt a few hours later, all the blood was gone. In all the confusion we hadn't noticed the shirt Reuben had been wearing during the incident. On the front of the shirt was written "Rock Solid in Jesus" and on the back the words "The wise man builds his house upon the Rock." We were reminded that the foundation of our faith was Christ, and that the angry rocks of the intifada could not destroy it.

It took a few days for our family to recover from the shock of what had happened. The coping techniques we had developed for the days of the intifada needed revising. We had told ourselves that if we stayed away from certain areas and traveled only in our self-designated "safety zones," nothing would happen to us. Lindell and I decided to replace the glass in our van windows with an unbreakable Plexiglas that would deflect stones and bullets. We even asked our children if they wanted to move to an area that might be safer, but they all agreed that we should stay in our new apartment.

God did not leave us alone during those emotionally low days. Throughout that week, friends and neighbors stopped by to tell us they were sorry this had happened. They delivered gifts of candy and toys to Reuben. Arab pastors came to comfort and pray with us. There was an outpouring of love and concern that brought healing to our discouraged hearts. Their love helped us as we explained to Reuben why faceless strangers had thought of him as an enemy and wanted to hurt him.

Through this incident, we learned again how God can turn evil into good for His purposes. We were able to share with our unbelieving friends how God had intervened and so the injury had not been serious. God led us to forgive instead of harboring bitterness and kept us "rock solid in Jesus."

5
THE GULF WAR

IN AUGUST 1990, during the middle of the intifada, a conflict began that would affect the whole world but especially the people living in the Middle East. President Saddam Hussein of Iraq invaded Kuwait and threatened to start a war that would be the apocalypse everyone feared. Our family had been in Cyprus during the time of the invasion, and we returned to a country that was anxious and frightened.

Americans living in the country of Jordan immediately felt the tensions increase. Many Arabs living in Jordan were strong supporters of Saddam Hussein and openly demonstrated both support for the invasion and antagonism toward Americans. Just a few weeks after the attack on Kuwait, the United States Embassy in Jordan asked all American citizens to leave. At that time the Church of the Nazarene had no missionaries living there.

When Jordanian Nazarenes heard Saddam Hussein's threat to use chemical weapons against Israel, they relayed to us their concern for our family and the Nazarenes living on the Holy Land District. By early September, American citizens living in Israel were told to be very careful and avoid travel in the West Bank. No one knew what to expect.

The country of Jordan faced a tremendous refugee problem. Jordanians and Palestinians who had lived and worked in Kuwait, Iraq, and the Gulf began to return. In addition, thousands of Iraqis from Christian backgrounds fled to Jordan. The Protestant Evangelical churches saw the enormous need of caring for these people and formed a coalition of churches to help.

One of our Nazarene pastors, Afeef Halasah, was asked to coordinate this new compassionate ministry. Jordanian churches and Nazarene Compassionate Ministries donated money to assist with the refugee problem. The Evangelical coalition that was responsible for one of the tent cities provided more than food and shelter for these men, women, and children. They handed out gospel tracts and showed the *Jesus* film to thousands of people. When temporary housing was needed for some of the refugees, the Nazarene school in Amman moved some families into guest rooms that were available.

The World Mission Division began to call regularly to let us know they were concerned and were praying for us. Each week tensions increased. The sound of sonic booms and the whizzing noise of jet fighter planes made us aware that the Israeli Air Force was preparing for war. At that time, Brittany attended high school at the American school near Tel Aviv and lived in a Baptist dormitory for missionary kids during the school week. Since the

United States Embassy helps support this school, we hoped they would keep families and students aware of the situation. But it soon became apparent that no one knew what to expect or what to do if there were a chemical attack.

We laughed when we read a letter from the school telling parents that sophisticated surveillance equipment would give a five-hour warning before the launching of chemical weapons. Parents would have time to drive to school, pick up their kids, and get situated in a safe place. We knew that should missiles be fired, pandemonium would take over, and it would be impossible to drive anywhere.

Our children were concerned, but one morning was particularly upsetting. It was the same day the government announced that gas masks would be distributed to everyone in the country. Lindsey, Erin, and Reuben were sitting in classrooms at the Anglican School in Jerusalem when the air raid sirens went off. There was confusion as teachers began to grab students and rush them into the bomb shelter. Some students began to cry. No one knew what to do. Fortunately, the alarm had accidentally gone off while being repaired. The incident made the seriousness of the situation a reality to the children.

By November, the hope for a peaceful solution seemed to be fading away. A phone call came from Dr. Robert Scott, then director of World Mission Division, telling us that the Security Management Committee had decided we should leave Israel for a safer place and wait there until the crisis was over.

When we told our children we might have to leave, they cried and begged us not to make them go. Lindell and I knew that no other mission organizations had evacuated personnel yet. If we left at that time, we would be one of the first families to depart. How could we leave our pastors and church people? We prayed together as a family and agreed we would ask to stay. After a lengthy phone conversation, Dr. Scott and the committee were convinced that we should wait. However, we agreed to leave if the United States Embassy advised American citizens to go or if other mission boards evacuated their missionaries.

There was something surrealistic about the possibility of a war using nuclear weapons, long-range missiles, and "smart" bombs. Those kinds of wars were fought on television screens, not in the country where you live. Although we were certain we had made the right decision, we wondered what we would do if war broke out. Lindell and I didn't want to risk the lives of our children. We prayed much and listened to every news broadcast we could find.

At Christmas celebrations and parties, nearly every conversation turned to a discussion of the likelihood of war. Some families left the country for the holidays, planning to stay longer if the war started. The city was devoid of tourists. War hung over it like a threatening cloud. The rumor spread that the United Nations was evacuating the dependents of their employees. The time had come for us to at least make reservations on an airline; that was part of our promise.

The day after we arranged a flight to Cyprus, the Israeli radio broadcast a long list of airlines canceling flights to Israel. Cyprus Airways was one of them. The few airlines that were still flying in and out of Tel Aviv had waiting lists with hundreds of names on them.

The younger children, Reuben and Erin, began to ask questions that revealed they were becoming afraid. What if they didn't know how to use their gas masks? What if they were at school when something happened? Our 8th- and 11th-grade daughters, however, still refused to think about leaving. We vacillated back and forth between our options. At one moment we would be certain we could not go; then a few hours later we decided we had to leave for the sake of our children. It seemed that no matter what we decided, it felt wrong.

I told one of our close friends that if a peaceful solution couldn't be negotiated, it was likely our family would have to leave. A look of sadness and disappointment came over her face. I didn't know what to say but finally asked the question, "Will your feelings about us change if we must go?"

She answered with more questions: "What about the people here? And what about the church?" There were no answers for her, and I left with a heavy heart.

In a final conversation with Dr. Scott, we asked if Lindell could stay in Israel if I left with our children. Dr. Scott understood our mixed feelings and sympathetically told us, "I will take the burden of the decision out of your hands. You must go." Our travel agent called to inform us that Olympia Airlines had not canceled flights into Tel Aviv, and he had managed to book us on a plane to Athens. From there we could fly to Larnaca, Cyprus.

Tearfully we said good-bye to our pastors and their families. Distraught faces revealed the fear they felt, but they comforted us with the words, "We love you, and we understand." Heartsick and weary, our family left the Tel Aviv airport on a midnight flight.

By midmorning we were opening the doors of the Nazarene Center in Cyprus. The Eastern Mediterranean Nazarene Bible College owns a fully furnished building that was unoccupied and available for us to use. On January 14 we arrived in Larnaca, and on January 18 at 2 A.M. the first Scud missile hit Israel.

Our family slept in front of the television and watched missiles fly through the air. We recognized buildings and streets and wondered if any of our friends had been injured. Lindell called Butros and Ramona Grieb, our pastors in Nazareth. Ramona answered the phone with a tearful voice that revealed the exhaustion of the past few hours.

Butros and Ramona had not slept since the first alarm went off. When the first Scud missile was fired, the faulty alarm system failed, and the police drove up and down the streets, using loudspeakers to waken and warn people that they were under attack. The Griebs' seven-year-old daughter began to cry, and the four-year-old wouldn't put on her mask. The baby was put into a special protective cot, but she cried the whole time and tried to get out. We knew they were extremely upset, frightened, and fatigued.

After the first attacks, all schools in Israel and the West Bank were closed. At least our children weren't missing school, we thought. Brittany was still angry about having to leave. The whole adult world upset her. Wars were adults' doing, and she resented the danger and disruption they brought to her and her friends. Rumors of how long the war would last ranged from six days to six months.

There were several missionary families from other organizations who also went to Cyprus. The Southern Baptist regional director asked us to join their missionaries as they talked about what had happened and about how to handle this stressful time. Realizing that all of us needed some structure to the long days ahead, Lindell and I offered to help set up an MK (missionary's kid) school in the classrooms we had available. We contacted our children's schools and asked them to fax us lessons for the kids.

Back in Israel, the panic of the first few weeks decreased, and schools reopened after a two-week closure. But people still lived in fear. Katy Tuma, the pastor's wife of the Jerusalem church, sent us the following fax:

> Good morning. We miss you all. How are you doing? It's boring here in Jerusalem; most of the people stay at home. They are scared to go

out. Now two nights have passed and nothing happened, but we still didn't sleep very well. Yesterday Nizar opened the church, but nobody came except one lady. We prayed together, then she left. We walked to the house of one of the church families and checked on them. We found most of their family there, so we had a meeting there. Nizar preached from Isa. 43.

Yesterday was the first time we went out shopping, but there was nothing to be found except bananas in the Old City market. We checked later in West Jerusalem and found everything we needed, but it was very expensive. The overall attitude in the country is bad; everybody is scared. The military has said the danger is still there and that we must take our gas masks with us when we go outside. Nizar called Butros [the pastor] and Nabil [director of the Nazarene school] in Nazareth. They are doing well. Butros had services yesterday and said about 60 people came. People want to pray, but most of the other churches were afraid to open.

We love you and miss you very much. Thanks for praying. We really feel the prayers working for us. Everyone says hello; they are waiting for you to come back.

Love,
Katy and Nizar

Even though our family was only a 45-minute flight away, it seemed as if we lived on another planet. We went to bed with our radios turned to the Israeli radio station so we could hear the attack warnings broadcast over the radio. After one such attack, Lindell called the director of our preschool in Nazareth. Thinking the attack was over, he wanted to see if everything was OK. Nabil Hakim's voice sounded muffled and strange as he told Lindell, "Could you call back later? We're under attack and have our gas masks on."

A month passed, and the war continued. Brittany grew restless and was ready to return soon after she heard her school had reopened. She begged us to let her go back with a Baptist missionary who had come from Israel for a few days of business in Cyprus. Eight-year-old Reuben was concerned about his sister leaving and what he should do. One night as I was preparing dinner, he came in to talk to me. "Mommy," he said, "I want to go back to Israel, but I don't want to go back if there might be more missiles. I'm afraid one might hit our plane." I knew we couldn't return yet, just as I knew we couldn't send Brittany away from the family.

It wasn't long after Brittany asked to go back that the ground war ended and the fighting stopped. Altogether, 39 Scuds had been fired at Israel, but only nine people had died from the war.* The nightmare had ended for our friends in Israel, and our family could go home.

When the war ended, we were among the first group of foreigners to return to Israel. Our pastors, church family, and friends warmly welcomed us back. They knew we had left with heavy hearts,

---

*Only one person died as a direct result of a missile attack. Others died from heart attacks or suffocation resulting from improper use of gas masks.

and their understanding spirits helped to heal our guilty consciences. The neighbor who had questioned our leaving greeted us with hugs and a warm welcome. Our children quickly settled back into school, although many students didn't return after the war. Somehow the Gulf War had changed us. We no longer felt home was back in the United States; home was the little apartment in the Jerusalem suburb of Beit Safafa. Home was where God had called us to be.

6

TRADING THE CRESCENT FOR THE CROSS

AN AMBULANCE SPED PAST US as we drove down the main road of Bethlehem. When it stopped at a checkpoint, I recognized the red crescent emblem painted on the side of the van. The crescent, symbol of the Islamic religion, encircled the familiar red cross that is associated with humanitarian works around the world and gave it a very different appearance.

As we waited in line for the soldiers to check our passports, I thought about one friend who had been a Muslim and who had attended a Christian conference with Lindell and me and other Nazarenes from our field. Enjoying the freedom of being away from her Islamic environment, she had borrowed a simple gold cross to wear around her neck. The cross symbolized the change that Christ had brought to her life. She and many other Muslim believers* have traded the crescent for the cross. As I waited at the checkpoint, I prayed for her and the many Muslim believers who are scattered around the world.

Most of the members of the Church of the Nazarene in the Middle East come from Greek Orthodox or Roman Catholic backgrounds; only a few are converted from Islam. The penalty for conversion from Islam to Christianity is very severe. In fact, in most countries of the Middle East it is illegal for someone to convert. Even if the conversion is not made public, that person risks rejection, physical punishment, and, in extreme circumstances, death.

In 1991 Lindell was asked to work with our churches in Egypt, an Arab country whose population is 90 percent Muslim. On his first visit there, one of the church leaders met Lindell at the hotel and gave him a strict warning: "Be careful—we are being watched." Islamic extremists had been persecuting and killing Christians, despite the government's efforts to control the violence. The church has reason to be cautious. They also have reason to rejoice.

The persecution the church has suffered has brought revival, and there has been a movement of God's Spirit among the Muslims in Egypt. We heard stories of how young men and women were

---

*In the Holy Land we often call converts from Islam "Muslim believers," because "Muslim" is as much a cultural term as it is a religious one. The phrase is not meant to imply that they are still practicing their former, Islamic, beliefs.

forced to leave their homes after their families refused to accept their faith in Jesus Christ. Lindell and I have had the blessing of visiting with some of these believers. Several had similar stories about the trials they had faced.

A young man named Musa shared how he had been arrested and put in prison because he was considered an enemy of the state. Although he was ruthlessly questioned and physically tortured, he refused to deny his faith. The other prisoners watched his persecution, unaware that he was a believer. When they saw him reading a Bible that had been brought to him by friends, they were puzzled. Why would he, a Muslim, want to read the Bible? Musa answered their questions by telling them about the freedom he had found in Christ. After weeks of imprisonment, he was released.

Churches in Europe and the United States have asked Musa and his fellow believers to share their stories of persecution, but they politely declined these invitations. They knew that if they left their country, they would not be allowed to return. God had not released them from ministry in the Muslim society of Egypt.

One form this ministry takes is the maintaining of safe houses, places in which Muslim believers can hide from the secret police. Those being hidden away cannot work and pay for the food and shelter that is given them. The Egyptian believers who provide the safe houses feel blessed and happy that God has given them this ministry.

Lindell and I learned that many Egyptian converts from Islam had first heard about Christ while studying in a university. As students discussed social and political topics, these conversations often led to dialogues about religion. The Christian students were then able to speak about Jesus. Before they invite new students to a Christian fellowship meeting, these Christian students pray for a discerning spirit so they will invite only those who are sincerely hungry to know more about Christ. One such fellowship had over 30 young people who had experienced new birth in Christ.

One young lady who had been active in one of these fellowships became a close friend to Lindell and me. When we first met Rima, she was secretly practicing her faith and had not told her parents of her relationship with Jesus Christ. She told us how her life had changed. Rima began her university studies dressed in the attire of a religious Muslim woman. She wore a floor-length dress or coat and covered her head with a long scarf that hid part of her face. Although Rima's family wasn't considered religious, they did observe the Fast of Ramadan, the days of feasting, and occasionally read the Koran. Her parents didn't encourage Rima's religious fanaticism, but they felt it would do her no harm.

When Rima first heard of the Christian student group conducting religious discussions at her university, she saw this as an opportunity to argue and prove the supremacy of the Islamic religion. The believers patiently listened to her arguments, then challenged her to listen to theirs. They provided her with books to help answer her questions about

Christianity. Rima reciprocated by giving them books on Islam. As she began to meet more frequently with these young people, she realized there was something different about their lives. They had the joy and peace she had been looking for. Gradually, her desire to know Jesus grew stronger and stronger. But she thought that the hope of Jesus belonged to the Christians and that it was impossible for a Muslim to know Jesus in the way these Christians did.

When Rima told the group how she felt, they revealed that they were Muslims who had accepted Jesus as Savior. She was shocked, for she had assumed these students who knew so much about Jesus were from Christian families. In her mind it was incomprehensible that a Muslim would leave Islam for another religion. One by one, Rima's friends told her about their conversion experiences and the peace Jesus had brought to their lives. She was even more shocked when she heard there were thousands of Muslim believers in the Arab world.

Rima started to believe that maybe this Jesus had also died for her. The leader of the fellowship realized it was difficult for this strong-willed woman to relinquish her heart to Jesus, so he challenged her. "I will pray to Jesus," he said, "and ask Him to reveal himself to you and give you the faith to believe. You pray to Muhammad and ask that he show you the falseness of Christianity if what we have told you is not true."

On Sunday Rima agreed to attend a church service with her new friends. Her heart was heavy with the conviction of sin and a longing for peace. She sat in the church and prayed, "Jesus, if You are who You say You are, reveal yourself to me." The pastor stood and started to preach. But as Rima looked at him, she no longer saw the church pastor but someone whom she knew was Jesus. With arms outstretched, He looked at Rima and said, "I love you and died for your sins." She wanted to reach out to Jesus but couldn't make her arms move. Instead, His arms grew longer and longer as He reached out to her. Rima didn't notice the sermon had ended until her friend sitting next to her tapped her on the arm. Tears were running down Rima's face. She explained that she had just seen Jesus, and peace had come to her heart. The darkness of Islam had fallen away.

For a year, Rima was able to be part of the growing, exciting fellowship of Muslim believers. Even though it was dangerous, she was baptized as a testimony to her faith. When she completed her university studies, she knew she must return home and face her family. However, it was possible they would throw her out of her home or physically harm her when they discovered she had become a believer. It was particularly difficult for her to say good-bye to her friends, because she didn't know when she would see them again.

Although Rima's family was happy to have her home, they noticed she had changed. She no longer wore the garb of a religious Muslim woman, and she had lost her interest in studying Islam.

Other things were different about Rima too, but they couldn't determine what they were.

Rima knew she must tell her parents about her faith but was frightened to do so. She loved her family very much and didn't want to hurt them. She knew her rejection of Islam and acceptance of Christ as Savior would bring anger and shame to the family, so she prayed for the right time to talk to them.

When Rima told us about her conversion, she was experiencing great pressure from her family. They were becoming more and more suspicious of her. The only Christian fellowship she had was an occasional meeting with a Christian friend, and it was impossible for her to attend church services.

I asked Rima how she managed to keep her faith strong under such circumstances. She answered that she listened to a Christian radio broadcast that was aired late at night. While pretending to sleep, the tiny earphones of her radio made it possible for her to listen to the program. Even her young brother, who shared her room, wasn't aware of what she was doing.

I asked Rima what program she listened to, and she said, "The Voice of the Nazarene." This was the Nazarene Arabic radio program produced by World Mission Radio. Although we knew others who listened to the broadcast, we were happy and proud to know of its ministry in Rima's life.

As often as possible we met with Rima. We encouraged her to tell her family of her commitment to Christ. That day came, and her family responded with anger and accusations. Although they didn't send Rima away from home, she was emotionally and physically isolated from her family. For several days they forbade her to leave the house. She was told never to go to church nor tell anyone about her conversion. Her brothers and sisters mocked her faith and spoke with hostility about those who believed in Jesus.

During the next few months Rima's family tried to destroy her faith and persuade her to return to Islam. She hid her Bible and other religious books around the house, but when her mother found them, she tore them up. Despite the mental pressures placed upon her, Rima didn't turn back. She told her family, "I will never go back to the darkness of Islam."

Several years have passed since we met Rima, and she has remained strong in her commitment to Christ. Her family still does not allow her to attend church and has warned her against meeting with us or other believers. Rima longs for her family to know Jesus and prays that they will someday accept Him as Savior. One of her dreams is to study someday at a Bible college and live openly as a Christian. If her life is endangered, she may someday be forced to leave her home. But until then, we will keep supplying her with Bibles and transistor radios. And God will supply her—and the many others like her—with the courage and faith to persevere.

7
BLESSED ARE THE PEACEMAKERS

THE CHURCH OF THE NAZARENE in Nazareth is one of the strongest churches on the Holy Land District, and its Sunday School and youth group have been one of its major sources of strength. When we began our ministry in Nazareth, Lindell and I prayed that God would call some of the young men into the ministry. It was encouraging to see teens from the church invite their friends to attend the youth meetings and Sunday services.

Nizar Tuma was one of the young men who, once introduced to the church, started coming to all the services. Nizar's family were members of the Greek Orthodox Church and had never visited an Evangelical church nor known any born-again Christians. Nizar found the people of the church friendly and the atmosphere in the church caring. His church didn't have this same feeling, even in its youth group.

When Nizar's parents discovered that he was attending the Nazarene church, they told him he should stop. They were suspicious of this church of which they knew nothing. But since Nizar was 18 years old and working over 80 hours a week, they decided they should permit him to spend his free time as he desired.

After attending the church for a few months, Nizar responded to a message on salvation and accepted Christ as Savior. The focus of his life began to change. He told his family of his new faith, declaring that he knew he had made the right decision. They again warned him to be careful and not to let his church attendance interfere with his work.

In the fall of 1985, Lindell began to teach theological classes to several young men who had expressed an interest in the ministry. Nizar wanted to take those classes but didn't know if he could shorten his 14-hour workday. God answered his prayer when his boss gave him 4 hours off work twice a week and didn't decrease his salary. In 1986 Nizar used his vacation time to attend Bible classes at Eastern Mediterranean Nazarene Bible College in Larnaca, Cyprus. By the end of that summer, he knew God was calling him to become a pastor.

Lindell and I began to pray that Nizar would find a wife who was a strong believer and a Nazarene. At our summer camp Nizar met Katy, who had been attending the Nazarene Sunday School in the Old City of Jerusalem since she was a small girl. He began writing her letters and calling her every week; 14 months later they were engaged. When the Morgans retired and we moved to Jerusalem, it was decided that Lindell would become district superintendent and would assist Nizar as the pastor of Jerusalem First Church of the Nazarene. After Nizar and Katy were married in October 1990, they moved into the apartment above the church.

Nizar has a wide grin that quickly makes people feel comfortable. He is an extrovert who can use his ability to speak Arabic, English, and Hebrew to witness to people. One of his greatest burdens has been to see reconciliation between Jews and Arabs, and God has been using him in this ministry. Since the Christians feel that the process of reconciliation must begin first among the believers and their leadership, Christian leaders in Jerusalem have asked Nizar to help bring together Arab believers and Messianic Jews. It is a ministry that has been challenging and fulfilling.

On the top of the Mount of Olives is a building called the House of Prayer, which is dedicated to prayer for the people of the Middle East. The building has provided an opportunity for Arab and Jewish pastors to join together for times of intercession. Nizar often attends these meetings.

One evening as they met together and shared the breaking of bread, Nizar was so moved by a spirit of love that he felt he must show his brothers in the Lord how much he cared for them. After speaking just a few words of explanation, Nizar went to the kitchen, filled a basin with water, picked up a towel, and returned to the room. He asked his friends to remove their shoes and socks; then he began to gently wash the feet of each one. Agape love filled the room as these men realized that they truly were brothers in Christ. When Nizar finished, one of the Jewish pastors washed Nizar's feet. Although these men had different political views, they were experiencing the peace that Jesus brings to His children.

Nizar is also involved with a group called Musallaha, which organizes teaching sessions and social activities to promote mutual understanding and friendship between believers from two peoples who have been at war for generations. Many of these young adults come with anger and bitterness in their heart toward each other. One of the best ways to get them to focus on the need to forgive has been to take them away from the city for retreats in the desert. On these trips they learn that they need to trust and depend upon each other for survival. Barriers are broken down, and reconciliation begins to take place.

One night as the group gathered around a campfire by the Red Sea, they began to confess to each other. Nizar told them that he had one time thought Jews had no right to become followers of Jesus. After all, they had rejected Jesus once, many years ago. Nizar then asked for their forgiveness for this attitude. Then a young man who had served in the Israeli army confessed to Nizar his hatred of all Arabs. While serving on the West Bank, this soldier had mistreated and been cruel to Arabs. He embraced Nizar and asked if he as an Arab could forgive him. The barrier and dividing wall of hostility came down.

One of the most exciting times of reconciliation came when 20 Jewish and Israeli Arab families traveled to Jordan to have fellowship with Jordanian believers. Two years earlier, no one would have imagined the borders between Jordan and Israel would open, and the cold war would end. Nizar and Katy were part of the group that traveled across the newly opened northern border crossing in order to share in this time of rejoicing and fellowship. They had found unity as Jews and Gentiles in the new covenant that Jesus inaugurated with His blood.

Nizar has used his Bible school studies to help him teach religion to Palestinian boys living at a boarding school in Beit Jella. These youths are children of the intifada and harbor much bitterness and hatred, and the message of reconciliation is not one they want to hear.

In a school north of Jerusalem, Nizar has been teaching Hebrew to 9th- and 10th-grade students. When he began teaching, he asked students why they wanted to learn Hebrew. One said it was because Hebrew was a nice language. Another answered she thought it would be easy to learn, since it was similar to Arabic. But one angry young boy replied, "Because it is the language of our enemy."

Before Nizar started his lesson, he told the students, "The only enemy you have is Satan. You need to learn Hebrew to help you understand the other people who live in this land. Jesus teaches us that we don't have the right to hate and do harm to those who are against us."

Nizar continues to use his gifts for God and spread the gospel message. He tells people that Christ is our Peace and that if we follow Him, then one day we will all be one.

8
EXILES FROM BABYLON

AFTER THE GULF WAR ENDED, Iraqi refugees continued to flood into Jordan. Some left the country because basic commodities were either unavailable or unaffordable. Others fled because they were afraid of the future under a government ruled by Saddam Hussein. Many of these people were from Christian backgrounds and had suffered under the domination of Islam. The future seemed dark, and people were desperate.

When I traveled to Jordan, I was anxious to meet these refugees. What would cause someone to leave a stable job and the shelter of a comfortable home for a crowded tent or a one-room apartment? A young Iraqi woman in our Nazarene church explained to us why so many people had run away from their homeland. The main reason was that a primary goal of the Hussein regime was to build a strong, united Islamic state. Even though nearly 95 percent of the population of Iraq is Muslim, there is a concerted effort to undermine the Christian religion. One Iraqi Christian was asked if she ever read the Bible. Her answer was, "What Bible? We only know that someone named Jesus was born."

The few Christians who attended church services knew nearly nothing about Christianity. The Iraqi government pushed its political ideas and Islamic principles on the Christians through the public educational system. It became apparent that if someone wanted to have a future in Iraq, he or she must accept the practices of the government, including those policies that discriminated against non-Muslims. Christians became so despondent that they were willing to pay a year's wages to obtain the exit permits needed to leave the country. Most families could not afford to send the entire family at once, so husbands and wives and even parents and children would be separated for months or possibly years.

Lindell and I were proud of our churches in Jordan. Nazarenes there reached out to these people in very tangible ways by providing food, shelter, and blankets. They realized that the refugees were spiritually starved as well as hungry for food, so church members invited them to the meetings. Our pastors and wives not only opened wide the doors of the church but also opened the doors of their homes and hearts.

Um Abee is the widow of Rev. David Nazha, who pastored the Jabal Church of the Nazarene in Amman for over 30 years. For many years she has led a weekly Bible study that ministers to both the younger and older women of the church. Even after her husband died in early January 1991, just before the start of the Gulf War, she continued these meetings. When the Iraqi refugees started coming to church services, she didn't hesitate to invite the ladies to this Bible study.

One of the most faithful to attend the Bible study was an Iraqi named Esther. Even though she lived far from the church, she seldom missed any meetings. When a church retreat was planned, she especially wanted to go. However, she couldn't leave her young daughters at home, and she didn't have the money to bring the girls to the retreat. Um Abee felt so strongly that God wanted Esther at this retreat that she asked the church board if they could pay for the girls to attend the retreat.

That weekend became a turning point in Esther's life. The speaker spoke clearly about a personal relationship with Christ, and Esther's heart hungered to know Him in such a way. After a morning service, Um Abee invited Esther to sit with a friend, and they talked about the things that troubled her. Esther shared her concerns and then told them about the desire she had to know Jesus. Um Abee attentively listened and then said, "Let's pray about all this." As the women prayed, Esther began to cry and also pray.

Suddenly she looked up and excitedly told the two women, "I believe the Lord is with me. I believe He will make a way. I believe!"

The women rejoiced together in the sweet presence of Jesus. They went to the next meeting together, where Esther shared what a change she felt in her life. She told those gathered in the service, "I don't know what has happened, but my heart has changed. Jesus is in my heart." She returned to her home willing to serve the Lord.

Esther couldn't wait to tell her husband, Esam, what had happened at the retreat. Sometimes he attended the Nazarene church with her, and she knew he was searching for meaning in his life. She dearly loved her husband, all the more so for what he had sacrificed for her.

Esam was born a Muslim and had done the unacceptable by marrying a Christian woman. Iraq had the same laws as other Islamic countries—a Muslim man can marry a Christian woman only if she converts to Islam. If the bride will repeat the *shahadi* (the pledge to the prophet Muhammad), marriage is permitted. Esther had said the shahadi but held on to her Christian heritage. Whenever possible she attended the Catholic church, and sometimes Esam went with her.

Esam was disillusioned with Islam and was looking for answers in Christianity. Sometimes he and his wife would read the Bible together as they searched for a way to put meaning into the chaos around them. When the secret police learned that Esam occasionally attended a Christian church, they threatened him with the loss of his job.

As an engineer Esam made a good income and provided his wife and daughters with a lovely, big home. But all that didn't matter to Esam. He was tired of living under the restrictions of Iraq. After the war, the family wanted to leave and had enough money to pay for the expensive travel permits. The emigration authorities granted permission for Esther and the girls to leave; but because Esam was a Muslim, he was not allowed to leave Iraq. That did not stop Esam. Even though it was dangerous, he fled from Iraq to Jordan without government permission.

Esam noticed a change in Esther after she came from the retreat. She was full of joy as she told what had happened. He began to attend nearly all the church meetings with her. In the church there was both a piano and an organ, but often there was no one to play them. Esther told Um Abee that in Iraq her husband had played the guitar and piano for wedding parties and other celebrations. Esam didn't know any hymns, but she could give him a hymnbook. He could practice and learn to play them for the services.

Esam agreed to this arrangement and began to practice. Sometimes he would come two hours before the service to practice on the organ. Alex Gazell led the singing in the service and came early to help Esam learn the hymns. During these practice sessions they began to talk about the Lord. Esam shared with Dr. Alex how he had been drawn to Christ in Iraq. Just a short time after Esther came back from the retreat, they prayed together for Christ to come into his heart.

There was rarely a service that Esther and Esam missed. The organ music was beautiful, and the congregation loved to hear him play. Esther was never too shy to pray in the meetings or share her testimony. They loved their church very deeply.

When their daughters started attending a

Christian school for Iraqi refugees, they were told the whole family must attend the church that operated the school. Esam explained to the school principal this wasn't possible, since they attended the Jabal Amman Church of the Nazarene. The principal sent a message to Esam and Esther threatening to dismiss the girls from the school if the entire family didn't come to their church. Most other schools wouldn't accept Iraqi children, so this was a serious concern. But Esam stood firm and told the school principal, "I'm not going to change my church for the sake of my children." The administration reversed their decision and allowed the girls to stay in the school.

In Iraq, Esam's work as a government engineer provided his family with a comfortable lifestyle, but in Jordan they lived much differently. Still, they were more fortunate than many, for they had not used all their savings to buy the expensive travel permits. When they left Iraq, they planned to be in Jordan for only a few weeks. Esther had family in Australia, and they hoped to immigrate there as soon as possible.

That immigration was not going to be easy. The family needed new passports to travel; but because Esam had illegally left Iraq, they couldn't go to the Iraqi Embassy. They could apply for Jordanian passports, but since Esam was from a Muslim family and Esther from a Christian family, they knew the government would not give them passports. Their case was presented to the United Nations department that deals with refugee problems.

After a review, the United Nations accepted their application for special travel documents. Esther could hardly wait to tell Um Abee and the whole church what the Lord had done. A few months later the family traveled to Australia, and one of the first things they did was look for a church.

Um Abee dearly misses Esther and Esam and loves to tell how God worked in their lives. After they had settled in Australia, Esther wrote Um Abee: "We thank the Lord because you showed us the right way to know Jesus. We wouldn't have found the Lord if we hadn't come to this church."

The church is a shelter for those who are weary and beaten down in a chaotic, sinful world. Sometimes those needing refuge can't get to a church. They are trapped in bomb shelters, prison cells, or even their own homes. But God provides for His own and lifts them above the discouragement and trials of life. "For in the day of trouble he will keep me safe in his dwelling; he will hide me in the shelter of his tabernacle and set me high upon a rock" (Ps. 27:5).

9
SOME THROUGH THE FIRE...

I PICKED UP THE RINGING PHONE, happy to hear Lindell's voice on the other end. He was calling me from Jordan, where he had just arrived after conducting a district assembly in one of the neighboring countries.* During this particular trip, General Superintendent William Prince was to meet Lindell in a northern city and conduct the assembly. Neither he nor Dr. Prince expected this to be an ordinary meeting, since one of the ordained ministers on that district was being held in prison on false charges. During the assembly they planned to spend most of the day in intercession for the pastor.

Lindell's first words to me were "I've got wonderful news! Brother Gabriel has been released

---

*Israel does not have diplomatic relationships with several of the Middle East nations, and no phone or mail connections exist where there are no diplomatic relations. Lindell and I cannot contact each other during Lindell's visits to some of the districts, so I am always anxious to hear from him after one of these journeys.

from prison. He got out the same day as the assembly, and we had a celebration instead of a business meeting." As Lindell, Dr. and Mrs. Prince, and Franklin Cook walked into the host pastor's home, they fully expected to find troubled, saddened faces. Instead they saw a table spread for a feast, filled with Arab dishes served only on special occasions. They were greeted with the news "Guess who's joining us for dinner? Brother Gabriel has just been released."

On a warm, sunny day in July 1994, Brother Gabriel had left his home for the long drive to the city, where he was to appear in court. He had been asked to give testimony concerning a legal matter, a confusion over property registration. But the questioning took a direction he didn't expect, and by the end of the session he found himself sentenced to jail.

Somehow Gabriel managed to stay calm and asked the judge, "If I must go to jail, don't put me in a place with murderers and thieves. You know I've committed no crime." Remarkably, Gabriel was sent to a jail that was fairly clean and organized. He did find it difficult to sleep at night, however, since his flimsy cot was located in a busy corridor. When one of the younger prisoners noticed his predicament, he insisted on giving Gabriel his bed in a small room, and he took the cot on the hallway floor.

When we first heard Brother Gabriel had been put into prison, we were greatly concerned. There was nothing tangible that Lindell and I could do to help. Even if we could obtain visas to this Arab country, a visit to the prison by Americans might make the situation more difficult for Brother Gabriel. A tall, handsome man in his mid-50s, Brother Gabriel was not in good health at that time. We wondered how he could handle the hardships of prison life. An urgent request was sent to the Prayer Mobilization Line of the Nazarene World Mission Society, asking Nazarenes around the world to pray for his release.

The greatest concern Gabriel had in prison was the burden his wife and church carried. Silwa, his wife, was shocked when she learned the court had sent her husband to prison. She cried out to God, questioning how something like this could happen to someone who had served Him so faithfully for so many years—the church needed him. She knew that those who had lied about her husband and brought about his imprisonment could make problems for the church. Immediately the church board organized a special time of intercession for Brother Gabriel. Every morning they went to the church and prayed for his release. Those prayer meetings became a source of strength for Silwa.

The weekly trips Silwa made to visit her husband in jail were both physically and emotionally exhausting. The journey took four hours by bus or taxi; and when she arrived at the prison, she had only a few hours with her husband. As a pastor's wife, she never expected to visit her husband in a jail. Nothing prepared her for the humiliation and discouragement she felt as she waited in line with the other visitors before going through an interrogation and security check.

Silwa's first visit was the most difficult. Her dignified, well-groomed husband walked into the visiting area, wearing dreary prison pajamas. She spoke to him through prison bars. Brother Gabriel tried to lift her spirits and never complained. He reminded her of the words of Ps. 23—his God was with him in this valley.

Gabriel spent much of his time in the jail reading his Bible. He asked Silwa to bring him more Bibles, and he began distributing them to the other prisoners. Some began to read the Word of God and started to ask Brother Gabriel questions. This gave him the opportunity he needed to tell them about the change God had made in his life. He shared his testimony and told them how God had saved him from a life of sin.

Gabriel had been born in a nominal Christian home, but his parents were not believers. In fact, his father struggled with alcoholism and died when he was only 45 years old. Even though Gabriel saw his father's addiction and the pain it caused his family, he followed in his father's footsteps and became a teenage alcoholic.

The worldly life attracted Gabriel, and he made plans to become rich and powerful. One of his cousins was a believer who tried to get Gabriel to attend church. He occasionally attended church with him but only because he enjoyed arguing with the preacher about the existence of God. His cousin didn't give up, however, and asked Gabriel to stay in his home for a few days when he came for a visit. Gabriel accepted the invitation with the understanding that he was free to drink if he wanted to.

On the first day of his visit, a pastor came by to call on the home of his cousin. He began to talk about Jesus and the power Christ had to change our lives. Gabriel's life of sin had not made him happy, and his addiction to alcohol was making him miserable. The pastor reminded him of what he knew—that God wanted to forgive him if he would confess his sins.

When Gabriel started to argue with the pastor, the words wouldn't come out of his mouth. The power of conviction moved upon him; and instead of arguing, he repented and asked the Lord to accept him. From that day on there was a radical change in his life. He had once told his cousin, "When I believe in something, I want to do it wholeheartedly."

Gabriel returned home and found a Nazarene church to attend. He began to witness for the Lord and helped with Bible studies and Sunday School. It was at this church that he heard about sanctification and the power the Holy Spirit gives for holy living. He consecrated his life to Christ and made himself available for ministry in the church. After studying and serving in the church, he one day became a Nazarene pastor.

Gabriel shared his testimony of God's grace several times in the prison. Some of the prisoners began to believe in the power of Jesus to change lives. The story Brother Gabriel told was quite different from the other tales they heard. Often they entertained each other with detailed stories about the crimes they had committed, but Brother Gabriel told them about the One who loved the criminal.

Silwa had contacted a lawyer about Gabriel's situation, and he immediately began to try to get him released. But the days turned into weeks and then months. Silwa contacted the lawyer almost daily, hoping to hear good news, but his usual reply was "Maybe next week."

One morning during his morning devotions, Gabriel felt the Lord tell him to prepare to go home. So he packed and cleaned up, waiting to hear he was free. A few hours later, guards came and told him he could go home.

As Brother Gabriel sat and drank a cup of coffee with Lindell, he told him what he had learned during his three months in prison. First of all, he had learned to trust more in God. Then he said he had a greater burden to tell those whose lives are captive to sin about the freedom Christ can give.

"I will tell them about the jail of condemnation after the Judgment Day," Brother Gabriel says. "You'll be locked away from loved ones and from God in heaven. Unless you've been in jail, you wouldn't understand what that is like. I will plead with those who aren't right with the Lord to repent."

In coming out of the prison, Brother Gabriel had only one regret. "I got out of jail just a little too soon," he said. "My time there wasn't long enough, because I was able to lead only two men to the Lord."

Gabriel thanked Lindell for the prayers of his

Nazarene brothers and sisters around the world and welcomed him to the banqueting table, where he told everyone there about the banner of love and protection God had provided.

10
OUTREACH TO THE MOON

ALTHOUGH THE WORK of the Church of the Nazarene in the Middle East began in the 1920s, it was not until 1991 that the Nazarene radio broadcast was initiated. Realizing that the most unevangelized areas of the world are the Muslim areas, the Church of the Nazarene decided to send the Good News message in the Arabic language across the airwaves of North Africa and the Middle East. Rev. Jacob Amari accepted the position as director of the Arabic radio broadcast in 1992.

Hours of preparation went into the planning of the Arabic radio program. Brother Jacob traveled to Monte Carlo to receive training from Trans World Radio in program production. Sermons were recorded and edited for future broadcasting, and a method of follow-up was developed in anticipation of listener response. As the day of the first broadcast drew near, publicity was sent to the Nazarene churches on the Eastern Mediterranean Field, encouraging them to listen to and pray for the broadcast. On April 1, 1993, the first Nazarene broadcast in Arabic was aired.

No one knew what to expect. Unfortunately, the Nazarene program was scheduled for the late hour of 11:45 P.M. on Monday nights, not exactly a prime-time slot. Still, good reports came in from our Nazarene listeners. They were proud and pleased to hear the voice of a Nazarene preacher on their radios.

In just a few weeks correspondence from listeners started coming in to Brother Jacob's mailbox. At first, most of the letters came from Egypt and Jordan. Many of the listeners were Muslims interested in knowing more about Christ. They asked questions about the crucifixion of Christ, sometimes challenging Brother Jacob's statements with arguments from Islam. As quickly as possible, Brother Jacob would answer the letters and send them Christian literature that explained the plan of salvation. Lindell and I rejoiced over the response to the Nazarene radio program.

Brother Jacob longed to meet personally with some of the people he regularly corresponded with, and it had become apparent to him that some of the Muslims were true followers of Christ and had accepted Him as Savior. Often their letters expressed the loneliness and isolation they felt in their homeland.

In strict Muslim countries, the only churches that are legally permitted to conduct services are those that minister to the expatriate community. Those who attend the meetings are Americans, Europeans, Indians, and Asians, but few if any are from the local population. Underground churches may exist, but often the new believers don't know about them or are afraid to attend. In countries such as Saudi Arabia, conversion from Islam to Christianity can be punished with death. The "Voice of the Nazarene" radio program became the spiritual lifeline for many of the listeners.

Each time we spoke with Brother Jacob, he talked about visiting some of these countries and finding the new believers who wrote to him. When talking over the phone about the possibility of a trip to the country of Yemen, he chose his words carefully. There's always the concern that others may be listening in on the conversation. Even when speaking in the privacy of his home, Brother Jacob would speak in hushed tones and use a coded language. Lindell and I would smile as he told us, "I need to go to the moon. When do you think I can go? Why don't you go with me?" I knew, of course, that they weren't dreaming about becoming astronauts but were planning a trip to this Middle East Muslim country.

It was nearly a year after the first broadcast that Brother Jacob made his first visit to the country of Yemen. One of the listeners to the Nazarene program was a Yemeni journalist married to an engineer. She and her husband invited Brother Jacob to stay in their home, for they wanted to have their two young daughters learn more about Christianity. While the Muslim parents sat nearby and listened, Brother Jacob would teach the girls about Jesus. Although the father faithfully prayed to Allah five times a day, he seemed interested in Brother Jacob's ministry. He even used his car to drive Brother Jacob to the home of other radio listeners living in their city.

Sometimes Brother Jacob would travel by bus for eight hours to meet and visit with listeners. It was thrilling for him to meet those from whom he had received letters. A young man named Nihad amazed Brother Jacob with his knowledge of the Bible. He knew from his own personal studies that when the disciples followed Jesus, they were baptized. So he asked Brother Jacob if he would baptize him as a follower of Christ. In a remote beach beside the Red Sea, Jacob baptized Nihad. After his baptism, he asked Brother Jacob to tell him all there was to know about the Church of the Nazarene. Brother Jacob sent him a simple book that had been translated into Arabic. Nihad embraced the doctrine of the church and now proudly calls himself a Nazarene.

Another Yemeni radio listener contacted Brother Jacob when he was visiting Jordan. He explained that he lived and worked in Saudi Arabia and listened every week to the Nazarene program. He also wanted to be baptized, so Brother Jacob and missionary Randy Owens arranged for his baptism at one of the Nazarene churches in Amman.

A few months later, Brother Jacob baptized a third Muslim believer. A young Iraqi woman named Zayna had contacted Brother Jacob and asked if she could meet with him and his wife,

Miriam, when she came to Amman. She came to the office with an Iraqi believer who was eager to have someone speak to Zayna. After Zayna explained that she had been listening to the program for months, she told Brother Jacob she had had a hungering in her heart to know more about Christianity ever since she was a little girl.

Brother Jacob began to explain the teachings of the Bible to her, starting with Adam and Eve and ending with Christ. She asked how she could become a Christian, and they prayed together in his office. He invited her to attend one of the Nazarene churches. Not long after she became a believer, she asked to be baptized as a testimony to her new life in Christ.

After Brother Jacob's trip to "the moon," he began to receive even more letters of response. Some months he received as many as a hundred. It is obvious that God is moving in miraculous ways. Brother Jacob says that many Muslims feel their religion and their political systems have failed to meet the needs of the people. In countries where there has been civil war, the ruling governments have not had time to monitor Christian activity, and there is actually more freedom for people to examine Christianity. Our Nazarene radio program was started at a strategic time and is touching the lives of hundreds of Muslims in countries that close doors to Christian missionaries.

After his first visit to Yemen, listeners would write Brother Jacob and ask, "When are you coming again? We need to see you." So another "moon journey" took place. This time Brother Jacob's goal was to bring together the various listeners around the country for fellowship and prayer. With suitcases packed full of Christian literature and Bibles, he flew to Yemen.

After settling in a hotel, Brother Jacob contacted Nihad and the other believers he had met on his previous visit. Most of these believers were young men, 18 to 30 years of age. They are secret believers, privately practicing their faith, and the problems they face are similar. Often they publicly confess their faith to their parents when the family is trying to force them to marry a Muslim. Even without the guidance and support of a local church or pastor, they know it is important to marry one who shares their faith in Christ. Angered parents would often reject this new faith and send the young man out of the home. They are cut off from family and live their faith without the support of Christian fellowship.

But Brother Jacob set out to change this isolated situation. One by one he visited or called the believers who had written him. He asked if they could travel and meet at the home of one of the believers for a time of fellowship. Over 23 came together and greeted each other with the warmth and hospitality characteristic of the Arab culture. They shared their testimonies of faith, prayed together, and departed as brothers in the Lord.

During one of our recent visits to Amman, Brother Jacob proudly showed Lindell and me pictures of these young men. We saw a photo of a Yemeni judge who had been baptized as a small child. His father had been a secret believer who wanted to raise his son as a Christian. The grown-up son, also a secret believer, longed to bring up his family as believers, but he had married an unbeliever and was concerned that his wife would divorce him when she learned he was a believer. Brother Jacob encouraged him to tell her about Christ by giving her books to read about Jesus and then talking to her about Him. "Gradually you will lead your family to Christ," he encouraged.

When the photos were put away, Brother Jacob carefully brought out an intricately embroidered piece of fabric from his briefcase. The craftsman had beautifully created a work of art that displayed the Christian symbols of a cross and lamb. Golden threads were sewn on the design, giving the illusion of light. Jacob told us that the man who had created this work of art owned an art shop in the market of the city. He made his living as a craftsman, famous for his embroidered wall hangings. This design was a special one that he had made for Brother Jacob. The craftsman proudly told Brother Jacob that this design symbolized Christ, whom he now chose to follow.

As the Nazarene radio program reaches into the untouched Muslim world, spiritually hungry Muslims are finding a peace and forgiveness unknown in Islam. The Islamic crescent is being illuminated by the light of the Cross.

CHURCH OF THE NAZARENE
3167 S. 10th
Independence, KS 67301

EPILOGUE

As I sat at the computer and worked on the final chapters of this book in April 1996, the news that came over the radio caught my attention. The Iranian-backed terrorist organization called Hezbollah was firing Katyusha rockets into northern Israel, and Israel was retaliating with "surgical" attacks in southern Lebanon and the city of Beirut. Immediately I thought about Lindell. He and Louie Bustle, director of the World Mission Division, had flown into Beirut that day. As far as I knew, they were still there. I prayed for their safety and hoped soon to hear from them. I struggled with the disappointment over the deterioration of the peace process. Hope for a better future seemed to be melting away as "cold" peace turned to "hot" peace and again to "no" peace. Then I reminded myself of Rom. 8:28—God uses all things for His purposes. He was in charge.

When Lindell called about 30 hours later, I told him how concerned for his safety I had been after I heard about the Israeli bombing on Beirut. He was shocked. They didn't know anything had happened. But after I relayed what I knew, we concluded that they had left the city just a few hours before the bombing began. Lindell explained they had taken a taxi across Lebanon into Syria and spent one night in Damascus. The next morning they rode in another taxi and arrived in Amman just in time for Dr. Bustle to speak at the special church service.

Of course, Lindell was eager to hear more information and soon learned that over 200,000 Lebanese civilians had fled cities in southern Lebanon and traveled north to seek refuge in Beirut. Within hours after he and Dr. Bustle had left the Nazarene School in central Beirut, thousands of people moved into the area of Sin-el-fil, where the school was located. The director of the school saw the crowded tents around the school and decided to help. Classes were canceled and the doors of the school opened to provide shelter for 350 people. Most of the "guests" were from non-Christian backgrounds. Nazarene Compassionate Ministries sent money to buy blankets and food, and again a cup of water was given in the name of Jesus.

But that's not all. Members of the church conducted a day camp to provide activities for the restless and frightened children. New Testaments were given to everyone, and over 50 attended the Bible study held at the nearby Nazarene church. Shelter and safety were provided, and Jesus' name was glorified.

The missiles stopped flying, and a cease-fire was negotiated two weeks later. The refugees returned to their homes. Undoubtedly, the missiles and bombs will fly again in some area of the Middle East. That's characteristic of the peace that governments and politicians provide. But God has placed a body of faithful believers who will be there to show the way to the shelter of His love and truth.